Watch for the Longest Day

by
Mark Nicholls

This first edition published in Australia in 2019 by:

Prahran Publishing
P.O. Box 2041, Prahran, Victoria, 3181

© Copyright Mark Nicholls 2019

Mark Nicholls has asserted his legal and moral right under the Copyright Act 1968 to be identified as the author of this work.

Published by arrangement with
Prahran Publishing, Australia.

All rights are strictly reserved.

No part of this publication may be reproduced, stored in a retrieval system or transmitted, in any form or by any other means, without the publisher's prior permission in writing. Copying of this script for performance reasons is also strictly prohibited by law, either in whole or excerpts from.

This book is sold subject to the condition that it shall not, by way of trade or otherwise, be lent, resold, hired out or otherwise circulated without the publisher's prior consent in any form of binding or cover other than that in which it is published and without similar condition, including this condition, being imposed on the subsequent purchaser.

Every reasonable effort has been made to trace copyright holders of material reproduced in this book, but if any have been inadvertently overlooked the publishers would be glad to hear from them. The story, all names, characters, and incidents portrayed in this book are fictitious. No identification with actual persons past or present, places, buildings, and products is intended or should be inferred.

ISBN 978-1-922263-14-8 Paperback
ISBN 978-1-922263-15-5 eBook

Dewey: 822.4

A catalogue record for this book is available from the National Library of Australia

Performance Licensing and Royalty Payments

Mark Nicholls retains control of both the amateur and professional stage performance rights of this play. No unauthorised performance should occur without the express and written permission of the playwright.

Restriction of Alteration

There shall be no modifications of any kind to the play including deletion of dialogue (including objectionable language), changes to characters gender or names, title of the play or music without the express and written permission from the author.

Sound and Video Recordings

This play may contain stage directions to include the use of music, video or other sound recordings either in part or in whole. The author and the publisher have not sought the right to use such content and performance rights permission should be obtained seperately. Permission to record audio and video recordings of all performances must also be explicitly given by the author in writing.

Author Credit

Performance rights approval requires credit be given to Mark Nicholls as the sole and exclusive author of the play. This obligation applies to the title page of every program or other advertising material distributed in connection to this play. The author's credit should appear immediately under the title of the play on all published material, and alongside no other individual. Font size of credit cannot be less than 50% of the largest letter used in the play's title.

Please email info@prahran.press
for all performance enquiries.

Dedication

for Jean May Cuff and Dorothy May Hutton

About the Playwright

MARK NICHOLLS has been performing on various Melbourne stages since the age of six and has an extensive list of credits as a playwright, composer, singer, actor, producer and director. He is Senior Lecturer in Cinema Studies at the University of Melbourne where he has taught film since 1993.

He is the author of *Lost Objects of Desire: The Performances of Jeremy Irons* (2012), *Scorsese's Men: Melancholia and the Mob* (2004) and recently published articles on Italian Cinema, Powell and Pressburger's *The Red Shoes* and Sergei Diaghilev's celebrated company, The Ballets Russes.

Mark is a film critic and worked for many years on ABC Radio and for *The Age* newspaper, for which he wrote a weekly column between 2007 and 2009.

He lives in Melbourne with his partner, Ali Wirtz, and their two sons Oscar and Carlo.

Series Preface

I wrote these plays for only one reason, to perform them. I publish them here, therefore, somewhat reluctantly. They were never written to be read on the page by anyone but a treasured posy of performers that I trust to help me rescue them from it. They were certainly never conceived of as works of anything so respectable as literature. Nevertheless, I have found two reasons to overcome my reluctance and my usual roguish prejudice against readers and writers in favour of performers and punters. One reason is that putting these plays into print provides the opportunity for the most engaged of those who saw and heard them to revive and revise the experience. The other reason is archival. I wish to leave a permanent, if inadequate, record of the facts of their production over a decade, in a private space in Melbourne, for the benefit of both a small, dedicated paying audience, and for a smaller band of compulsive show-folk.

Writing these plays for the talented actors, musicians and backstage characters whose creations are recorded here, and having the privilege of working with these artists to produce them, has been the most satisfying occupation of my otherwise horrendously charmed and fascinating life.

Now that they have had their blessed release in print, these plays are beyond the concern of any motivation I had to write them. Read them, o curious one, and work it out for yourself! One motivation I will record, however, rests in the inspiration generously given by those who worked on and attended these cosy performances, and so brought their privileged, fleeting moments of theatre securely into being.

About the Play

In April 1927 the Melbourne *Argus* ran a story about my great-grandmother petitioning for Judicial Separation from my great grand-father. This story, about a woman shunning divorce from her clerical husband but seeking some sort of judicial validation for her desired separation, is, I suspect, curious to read for most people. From the tone of his comments I gather the poor magistrate thought so too. Clearly, were it not for the implied sex, the scandalous clerical element and a degree of collaboration between the petitioner and the court reporter on a slow news day, I doubt that the *Argus* would have bothered.

I never met either of this pair of great-grandparents and I knew very little of their history. I did know enough of its setting and something of the inclination of its protagonists not to find this report at all remarkable. What arrested me about it was that fact that my great-grandmother should haul her son, my grandfather, into court to give evidence against his father in this matter. I knew my grandfather very well and I liked him. He was kind and amusing and he always treated me with a degree of civility, which is often overlooked by one's familiars – as he knew very well. To see his young adulthood punctuated in this way, and in the public setting of what he once described to me as "a perfectly ordinary middle-class newspaper", made me grieve for him. I wondered what possessed his mother to put him through it and, indeed, to put herself through it.

If my grandfather suffered at all from his role in that affair, I never saw any evidence of it in the twenty-odd years I knew him. Quite ignorant of it all, I one day happened to ask him about his father. By that stage of his life he was far more concerned with enjoying a recent victory he had had over the grim reaper and those of us who had prematurely written him off. He obviously had little lasting concern for what had happened to his parents all those years ago. Nevertheless, asked the question, he smiled and blew me off with some sort of story about his father's alcohol-induced madness. In a family where booze was possibly worse than sex, I had no difficulty in swallowing his version of events and I left it at that.

I know nothing more about this little family tragedy than I knew then. Writing up their lives according to my own instinct and experience, perhaps valid in this case, I feel I know them all a little better and can largely excuse them their folly – whatever it really was. Some of the psychological impacts of World War One on all of them clearly seemed to have played an outsized role in their motivations. What I do find hard to forgive is the impact these events had on those unconventional women who married into this mess.

Hardly inclining to the informational over-share, one of these women, my grandmother, sat with me in the garden one Sunday after lunch and told me something of her young married life and the implied impact of her mother-in-law on it. Saying very little, the fact that she coupled her account with her grave concern for her three children and her patent sense of relief that they had survived it, told me a great deal about her substantial analysis of the situation. A brilliant woman, of very good sense and judgement, she probably deserved better then to be stuck with these crazy people and their petty, 'perfectly ordinary middle-class' problems. Perhaps her choice of in-laws questions her judgement. If this is one error in understanding she did make, however, with a great feeling of empathy, I can easily forgive her that. I have to because, without it, I would not be here to write our story.

Characters

Jennifer Bainbridge: thirtysomething.

Sarah Bainbridge: thirtysomething.

Alice Bainbridge: mid sixties

Henry Newman: aka, Henry Bainbridge, mid sixties

Jonathan Bainbridge: a teenager.

Setting

Summer 1948 in a quiet but seasonally busy seaside hamlet somewhere in Victoria.

Also, a court room in Melbourne, April 1927.

Act 1: Scene 1

It is morning. The lights come up on a small sitting/dining room with a table and chairs stage left, two uncomfortable chairs stage right in front of a modest fireplace. There is a small coffee table with a book or two on it, one of which is the Bible [black].

JENNIFER enters from the kitchen upstage left and is setting the table for breakfast. She is noticeably cheery. She is enjoying the quiet of the early morning, her solitude, and is relieved by the anticipated arrival of her husband later in the day. Music plays throughout her ritual.

The table is now fully set for seven. And JENNIFER has momentarily left the room. SARAH enters in a tidy and modest dressing gown. She takes a look at the table and rolls her eyes. As she perceives JENNIFER returning, she makes herself busy, rearranging things on the table. JENNIFER reenters.

JENNIFER: *[Waking out of her dream]* Oh. Good morning.

SARAH: *[Becoming noisy with the plates]* It's early to be setting up for breakfast. The children aren't even awake yet and Granny won't be up for hours.

JENNIFER: I know. I'm enjoying the tranquillity *[Taking a cup from her and lowering her voice]* which is why I'm being very quiet.

SARAH: Yes, well that's Granny's cup so it needs to go there *[the head of the table]* and Charles gets the bigger plate so that needs to go next to her.

JENNIFER: I thought we might have breakfast early this morning and then take it into Alice later on a tray.

SARAH: She won't like that. And I doubt she likes you calling her 'Alice' either.

JENNIFER: She doesn't mind.

SARAH: You never call her that to her face.

JENNIFER: Not exactly. I'm too scared. I never really know what to call her. But when you think of it, it's quite funny. After thirteen years of marriage I seem to have got away without calling her anything very much.

SARAH: So I've noticed.

JENNIFER: Yes. I dread the moment when I have to introduce her. But then I never have to introduce her because I don't know anyone, and she knows everyone.

SARAH: Just call her 'Granny'.

JENNIFER: I can't do that. I already have a 'Granny' and she's a lovely, caring and serene little woman who lives a long way away. No, I can't call her that. And I certainly can't call her Mrs Bainbridge. Perhaps I'll call her 'Mother-in-Law'?

Act 1 – Scene 1

SARAH: Do not call her that. And don't call her 'Alice'. For someone who seems so terrified by her you really can be quite impertinent with her at times. I suppose it is some sort of extreme nervous reaction and you can't help it. You would really do yourself much better here if you, I don't know, 'came to heel' a bit more. I'm sure if you did, she would have far less cause to find fault with you.

JENNIFER: I wasn't aware that she did.

SARAH: Well, she does. All the time. I try to put a word in for you, but you're too wilful. I can't make excuses for you indefinitely.

JENNIFER: Well, I don't want you to make excuses for me at all. If she dislikes me that is really none of your concern.

SARAH: It is my concern, because I have to listen to it. It's the same with your Sophie. You're too soft with her and she annoys Granny.

JENNIFER: There's nothing wrong with Sophie and I am not soft on her. And I am sick of having to scold her in front of Alice because you do it to your daughters. None of them is ever doing anything wrong. They're just normally high-spirited little girls who like to be noisy sometimes. Why does Alice have us here if she doesn't like children?

SARAH: She does like children. She adores Charles.

JENNIFER: Oh yes. She adores Charles. It's the same with Harry too. It is just the girls she can't stand. Have you ever known a woman who seems to hold such antipathy to her own sex?

SARAH: That is a grotesque suggestion. You're making much too much of it.

JENNIFER: Oh well, I suppose I will just have to continue to call her 'hey you' for the mean time.

SARAH: I'd like to see you try. Anyway, why do you want the children up so early? We don't have to catch a train.

JENNIFER: I thought of taking them to the beach early today so they can be back when Jonathan arrives.

SARAH: He won't want to be bothered with the children when he first arrives. I would leave them at the beach, if I were you, and give him a few minutes to relax before they start bothering him.

JENNIFER: They don't bother him. Why would he come at all if they bothered him?

SARAH: I'm sure you know. *[She makes for her room]* Anyway have an early breakfast with your children if you like but please don't wake mine. They were all up late last night and I don't want them tired and grumpy all day. Granny doesn't like it. *[She leaves]*

JENNIFER sits down exasperated. Lights fade.

Act 1: Scene 2

It is an hour later. JENNIFER is now clearing the table after the children have left. Eventually SARAH enters, now fully dressed.

SARAH: Where are the children?

JENNIFER: They all went off for a walk around the point.

SARAH: What?

JENNIFER: It's all right. It's low tide and Charles is with them. I gave them breakfast.

SARAH: I particularly asked you not to do that.

JENNIFER: I didn't wake them up.

SARAH: No, Sophie did when you woke her.

JENNIFER: I didn't wake anyone. And if anyone did bounce about a bit it was probably Charles. They all got up and came in together, and we had an unusually serene and enjoyable breakfast. They weren't grumpy or tired. In fact, they were all so charming that I forgot to make them do the dishes – no doubt confirming in your mind once-and-for-all that I am far too soft and, indeed, wilful. Did you enjoy an extra hour's sleep?

SARAH: No. I wasn't sleeping. I was mending.

JENNIFER: Well, I'm sure 'Granny' did. Did I say that correctly?

SARAH: Sarcasm really doesn't suit you, you know.

JENNIFER: I didn't mean to be sarcastic 'Sister-in-Law'. You see, as you know, I didn't grow up in Melbourne among gentle folk. I didn't go to Merton Hall. Only lately have I come under the benign influence of those kindly ladies of the Presbyterian Friends Association – I wonder whether there is an Enemies Association? – so, as you know all the right things to do, I'd be grateful if you would take it upon yourself to instruct me whenever it seems appropriate.

SARAH: Gladly.

JENNIFER: *[With a tray for ALICE]* Shall I take this into 'Granny' now or is it more seemly that the wife of the second son should do it? You don't think that as the wife of the eldest son and heir it might compromise my dignity?

SARAH: *[Taking it from her]* I'll take it into her. You are just being foolish.

As she does she bumps into ALICE entering and nearly spills the whole thing.

ALICE: Where on earth are you going with that Sarah Smith? Don't you know I abhor food in bedrooms?

Act 1 – Scene 2

SARAH: Yes, I do. But Jennifer insisted I bring it into you. She thought that you would consider it a kindness.

ALICE: She is grossly mistaken.

JENNIFER: *[Settling with the newspaper]* For goodness sake.

SARAH: Well, what should I do with it, Granny?

ALICE: Put it down on the table, remove the 'tray', reinstate the eating irons and restore the cup and saucer to their traditional breakfast-time habitation.

SARAH: Wouldn't you prefer me to reheat the water?

ALICE: No. I'll take it cold. Hot tea is the last sign of weakness and an intermediate sign of decadence. *[She sits at the head of an empy table]*

JENNIFER: Good morning... ah... 'Granny'.

ALICE: Good morning Jennifer. *[She stops to think]*. Why do you call me that? You've never called me that before.

JENNIFER: No. But I have never really called you anything before. What should I call you?

ALICE: Be inventive, young woman.

JENNIFER: I'll try.

ALICE continues with her tea, then stops to think again.

ALICE: Where are my grandchildren?

SARAH: They have gone off on a walk. Jennifer gave them an early breakfast.

ALICE: And why did she do that?

JENNIFER: She did it because her husband is arriving today, and she thought that the children might like a longer stretch at the beach before he does.

ALICE: Again, grossly mistaken. Unless my son has taken to telling his wife one thing and his own dear mother something quite different.

JENNIFER: What do you mean?

ALICE: I mean he is not arriving today or any other day in the next week.

JENNIFER: But he sent me a note about it a week ago. How long have you known this?

ALICE: For at least a week.

JENNIFER: And you didn't think of telling me?

ALICE: Perhaps I told Sarah.

JENNIFER: Why should you tell Sarah and not me?

ALICE: I really don't remember.

Act 1 – Scene 2

JENNIFER: Well, Sarah never mentioned it.

SARAH: I didn't want to interfere. Anyway, I thought perhaps there might be some point of tension between you. It felt awkward.

JENNIFER: You never even mentioned it this morning.

SARAH: Well, I thought perhaps he had reverted to his original plan. It's not really my business, obviously.

JENNIFER: Well that is really very disappointing. I was looking forward to seeing Jonathan and so were Sophie and Charlie.

ALICE: I really don't see what all the fuss is about. The last thing any woman wants is her husband away from his work and under her feet while she is trying to enjoy her holiday. I would have thought you might be relieved.

JENNIFER: I can't imagine why you would say that. He's your son after all. Don't you want him here?

SARAH: Granny was only thinking of you, Jennifer. You know how he grumbles when he has to break his summer work routine to come down here. I'm sure it's all for the best.

JENNIFER is yet again exasperated. The lights fade.

Act 1: Scene 3

JENNIFER is sitting on a bench on a small stretch of grass overlooking the sea. She is half reading the novel **Gentleman's Agreeement***, half watching her children on the beach.*

JENNIFER: Charlie *[Gesturing with her head]*... Sophie. *[She listens to him]* Yes. But don't let her know you are. I don't care if she can't do it on her own. I just don't want her to think she can't. She might surprise us. Go on.

She reads with a brief musical overlay. Eventually HENRY approaches.

HENRY: Excuse me. I'm sorry to interrupt your reading, but would you mind if I sat here? All the other benches are taken and I'm not really dressed for the sand dunes.

JENNIFER: Of course not.

HENRY: Please don't stop your reading. We don't have to speak. The view is so perfect on its own, we don't have to discuss it.

JENNIFER: Of course. *[She reads in vain]* I wish you hadn't said that. Now I don't feel like I am allowed to talk, because, maybe you don't want to and, if I do, I am being forward or something.

HENRY: No. I was just being polite. Please talk if you feel the need.

JENNIFER: I know you are being polite. But that just makes me wonder if you are really quite rude, deep down inside, and now you are just on your very best behaviour.

HENRY: I hardly know what to say now. I think it would be best if you did the talking.

JENNIFER: It's a lovely day.

HENRY: It is. Unseasonably mild for January.

JENNIFER: Yes.

They laugh.

HENRY: Which of those children is yours?

JENNIFER: That boy and that girl.

HENRY: They look pretty capable. You have no excuse for your lack of progress on that book.

JENNIFER: Perhaps I am savouring it?

HENRY: Believe me you're not. I've read it and it is by no means Proust.

JENNIFER: You're right. Actually, my daughter is still learning to swim so I am averaging about two sentences an hour.

HENRY: Her brother looks fairly reliable as a lifeguard.

Act 1 – Scene 3

JENNIFER: He is. But, at his age and according to his temperament, if a ball goes flying past, he's bound to leap for it and forget all about his little sister.

HENRY: I understand. Are you enjoying your holidays?

JENNIFER: To be honest, no.

HENRY: How unusual.

JENNIFER: Do you think enjoyment is mandatory at the seaside in summer holidays?

HENRY: No. It's unusual for anyone to admit it's not. Especially to a stranger.

JENNIFER: I'm sorry. Was that indiscreet? I am always putting my foot in it and saying the wrong thing.

HENRY: Not at all. Honesty is never anything but admirable.

JENNIFER: I am not exactly in my natural element in this part of the world. I think I am just getting the idea that when someone asks after your health here they really don't want an actual answer.

HENRY: You're quite right. But it does make us all sound just a little bit interesting when, in reality, we are not interesting at all. Unnecessarily complex perhaps, but not interesting.

JENNIFER: You don't think social complexity is interesting? Isn't it the height of sophistication?

HENRY: It may be, but it doesn't interest me, I'm afraid.

JENNIFER: Perhaps it is just that you have been pushed out of heaven?

HENRY: Yes, I have. I am beyond the pale. Almost a savage.

JENNIFER: You look civilised enough.

HENRY: Anyone can pass muster in a seaside resort if they can manage to appear and look like they didn't just come from a robust session in the garden. That is, if they are wearing anything very much at all.

JENNIFER: Now I am self-conscious. I am only just getting a hold of what not to say, now I have to consider what not to wear?

HENRY: I wouldn't bother if I were you. Anyone could tell by looking at you "that you don't give two hoots about what you wear".

JENNIFER: Thanks very much.

HENRY: I am obviously teasing. Didn't you see *Rebecca*? I hope you don't mind. You are clearly at the height of fashion. You might even be respectable.

JENNIFER: Now you really are trying to insult me. When I think of what passes for respectable in this place I think of *[looking around]* those elderly ladies sitting down there.

HENRY: Yes. They look as if they are off to a funeral.

Act 1 - Scene 3

JENNIFER: I admire their resilience. Their respectability is making absolutely no concessions to their activity. I doubt I could wear those outfits anywhere other than a morgue or funeral parlour. But there they are, lazing around on the beach, totally unconcerned. They don't even seem to be sitting on a towel. Whereas you, besuited but light and summery, won't even risk anything but the cleaner end of my bench. I'm sure those shoes would cope admirably, but I've no doubt that they have never been near the sand, ever.

HENRY: You are right. I never really became reconciled to wearing anything very much by the sea. Time was you could swim here most of the day without a stitch and no one seemed to mind very much.

JENNIFER: And then God created Eve.

HENRY: It wasn't as long ago as that.

JENNIFER: No, probably not. In your day the ladies probably stayed in the boudoir until three, took two hours to dress, appeared here at five and returned to their bath about twenty minutes later.

HENRY: It certainly wasn't as long ago as that. I may be old enough to have grown up children, but I am not that old.

JENNIFER: Perhaps.

Pause.

HENRY: Why are you not enjoying your holidays?

JENNIFER: I'm grumpy. I have been running around after my children since Christmas and running the gauntlet of several others too, and their mothers, and their grandmothers. I was expecting a little light relief today when my husband arrived. Only now I find he's not coming at all.

HENRY: That is disappointing. Does his work keep him busy elsewhere?

JENNIFER: I suppose so. Although he is probably just avoiding what I am complaining about here. Listen to me! I can't believe I am blurting all this out. I am indiscreet.

HENRY: I don't think so. In any case, it doesn't matter. We probably won't meet again for at least twelve months and by then you'll have been so busy dealing with all the business of life that you will have totally forgotten our conversation. And then, even if you do remember your indiscretion, I am expert in looking like I am so important and self-interested that you will think I was never really interested in what you had to say in the first place.

JENNIFER: Well, that is something of a relief. I think.

HENRY: May I ask what line of business you husband pursues?

JENNIFER: Oh, he does something in a bank in Melbourne.

Act 1 – Scene 3

HENRY: "High up in a bank or just in a little cage totting up things?"

JENNIFER: What?

HENRY: Sorry. It's a quote from a play. Way before your time.

JENNIFER: It did seem impertinently amusing.

HENRY: Have you been here before? I've never seen you.

JENNIFER: I have, but only just after my marriage when my eldest was very young. Not during the war.

HENRY: Holidays postponed for the duration?

JENNIFER: Not really. I moved to Mount Dandenong with my mother.

HENRY: To escape the Blitz.

JENNIFER: That was the idea. But it wasn't mine. Although I stayed there for as long as possible. I think I was the only person in the country who didn't want to discount the idea of a Japanese invasion.

HENRY: You were happy there?

JENNIFER: Yes, very happy.

HENRY: That is very agreeable. Can I ask you why? It can't have been easy in wartime.

JENNIFER: It was certainly simpler. I had my two children and my mother – and my husband came up every weekend. There was a small school for Charley and once we finally found him a piano to practise on we lived in complete contentment. It's almost disturbing to think of it now, but while all the most unspeakably horrible things were happening all over the world, we seemed to be living in the very best part of our lives. I felt so happy there and safe from harm.

HENRY: I think there are many stories like yours.

JENNIFER: I wonder what the men off fighting would have thought of all of us having such a good time.

HENRY: Well, I had to do that twice and all I can say is that if I thought my family were so content at that time I would have been grateful.

JENNIFER: Really? That's interesting.

Pause.

HENRY: I assume you are here for the month?

JENNIFER: Both months, actually. I'm here with my mother-in-law and her extended family, the Bainbridges. You probably know them, if you are here a lot yourself.

Act 1 – Scene 3

HENRY: Everyone knows everyone here. *[Pauses. He knew this but starts to feel uncompfortable and guilty]* I don't mean to be rude, but I have just remembered something I really must do. Would you excuse me? *[He gets up]*

JENNIFER: Of course.

HENRY: Please excuse me leaving so abruptly.

JENNIFER: Not at all.

HENRY: Goodbye.

He leaves.

JENNIFER: *[Watching him go]* Goodbye.

She turns again to watch the children as the lights fade.

Act II: Scene 1

As in Act One Scene One. SARAH is madly cleaning up the room obviously with something else on her mind. She is wearing clothes that indicate she has been to a function. Eventually ALICE enters.

ALICE: There seems to be a somewhat manic note to your tidying, Sarah.

SARAH: I don't really know exactly what that means, but if it implies that I am cross, well, I am.

ALICE: Why? And why are you dressed as if you are about to meet an intimidating old school friend for tea at George's Regency Room?

SARAH: Your critique of my costume choices seems to be more elaborate by the day.

ALICE: I wouldn't say elaborate. I would say efficacious.

SARAH: Then it's your vocabulary that is becoming more elaborate.

ALICE: What do you have to be cross about?

SARAH: I've been to the tea at the Deakin house with Charles and he embarrassed me terribly.

ALICE: What do you mean?

SARAH: It had been announced in the program that he was to play some Bach and some Mendelssohn. Well, do you know what he did? He sat down at the piano in front of three-quarters of the local society ladies, took one look around the room and then proceeded to give us all a lengthy recital of a lively selection from Gilbert and Sullivan!

ALICE: I suppose the Deakin women were horrified?

SARAH: No, that is just it. They were delighted. Some of them even indulged in a little foot tapping and a spirited sing-a-long.

ALICE: Outrageous. But it doesn't seem to me to be a serious offence.

SARAH: It was to me. I didn't take him there to show us all up as some sort of carnival act. I took him there to play some serious music.

ALICE: You are being far too sensitive about the whole thing. It sounds to me like he made quite a judicious selection. Anyway, I hardly think you need to worry about what concerns a few of the ladies who take tea at the Deakin house. *[Looking at her watch]* I expect if you hadn't rushed off so early you would have found that, no doubt, they would have served sherry!

SARAH: No one serves sherry here. That's far more Portsea. And I do concern myself with what people think of Charles, and of the rest of us for that matter.

Act II – Scene 1

ALICE: There is hardly anything irregular about a talented boy playing some light opera to a room of elderly ladies in a seaside salon.

SARAH: It is not Charles that is irregular, it's us.

ALICE: And how are we irregular?

SARAH: The way we live.

ALICE: And how is that?

SARAH: You know how we live.

ALICE: Well, you obviously think I don't. Otherwise you wouldn't be making such a fuss over the less *Well-tempered Clavier* and the odd *Song Without Words* with words.

SARAH: It doesn't always have to be said.

ALICE: But it is never said. It hasn't been said for twenty years. And that is the point. If I choose to live in this place and in this way, without my husband, then that is none of the concerns of the Deakin ladies, whatever you think. And if the Deakin ladies do waste their time thinking about it then it still makes no difference at all because, despite their salons and their sherry and their obvious lack of any sort of coherent and practical education, none of those ladies was brought up so badly that they would ever dare mention it.

SARAH: Their daughters do.

ALICE: I doubt that. Or at least they won't once their mothers get wind of it.

SARAH: It is not only about you.

ALICE: Well, what is it about?

SARAH: Well, the way Jennifer brings up her children and the fact that Jonathan is never here. It is all very unusual and makes this family look like a carnival.

ALICE: Be careful Sarah. It is starting to sound as if that jealousy of yours is rising up again. Are you sure Jonathan's summer activities would have been any different had he married you rather than Jennifer? It is not as if we are constantly blessed with the company of your husband either.

SARAH: That's ridiculous. That idea of me marrying Jonathan was your idea. Frankly, I think I always preferred Philip anyway. No, my concern is that we all look as if we have a general lack of control and restraint in this house. If you had established a bit more authority over your sons we might not be in the position we are now.

ALICE: Sarah, I advise you to avoid trying to be eloquent over matters that you don't understand.

SARAH: What do you mean?

ALICE: Well, I know you think it is all about you and how you appear to those particularly nasty young women you seem so intent on ameliorating. But, believe me, it's all far beyond that. It is about people and things that occurred well before you were even thought of.

SARAH: It hardly matters when it was. It is intolerable.

ALICE: I know that you are disappointed in us. You really were silly enough to imagine that you were getting something quite different in my family, which is why you agreed to marry Philip when you lost out on Jonathan.

SARAH: You really think me so calculating?

ALICE: Yes, I do, because I encouraged you.

SARAH: Well, then you agree that you have been lax when it comes to your responsibilities.

ALICE: I can't believe we are really making such a fuss over a few bars from *Iolanthe*.

SARAH: It is not about that and you know it. What you don't want to acknowledge is that there is something really wrong in this house. I'm trying to put the best face on it that I can and do the best to present us in a more acceptable light. Whereas you seem to want us all to luxuriate in our perversity.

ALICE: Is that why you met with my husband in Collins Street in November?

Pause.

SARAH: I wondered if you knew about that.

ALICE: There's not much I don't know about what goes on in Melbourne. Particularly in Collins Street.

SARAH: Well, why did you never mention it? That is exactly the sort of thing that is wrong in this family. Everyone sneaking around and keeping secrets.

ALICE: Well, you were sneaking around in order to meet my husband.

SARAH: I wasn't sneaking around. Philip knew all about it. I just never mentioned it to you. I can't see why you would object. You never say anything about him at all.

ALICE: That may be true about my not speaking of him, but you know very well why I would object to you meeting him.

SARAH: I don't as a matter of fact. Perhaps it is about time you told me all about it.

ALICE: I don't think so.

SARAH: Why not? What is so utterly disgusting about it that you feel you can't enlighten me?

ALICE: I am not going to be questioned about my marriage by you.

Act II – Scene 1

SARAH: Well, you can hardly expect me to me to decline an invitation from Mr Bainbridge simply on the basis of a vague disinclination on your part.

ALICE: My reasons satisfy me.

SARAH: You could at least name one of them.

ALICE: That man is beyond the pale. I deprecate any idea of you or any other member of this family having anything to do with him. I certainly don't want him discussed here and while I am running this house and paying the bills I expect to have my wishes respected.

Pause.

SARAH: Well, I suppose that's about it then.

ALICE: In any case, I wouldn't be too worried about what we look like, if I were you. Every family has its growing pains. Ours go back a long way and they will go on a lot longer. At least well beyond the scope of your young life. Come and see me in twenty years and see if you don't think the same thing.

Lights fade.

Act II: Scene 2

As in the previous scene. Two hours later.

JENNIFER: *[Off]* Leave the beach things outside, Sophie, and go straight into the bath. Sarah! *[She enters]* Sarah!

SARAH: *[Off]* I'm coming.

SARAH enters.

JENNIFER: Is Charles with you?

SARAH: He's in his bedroom.

JENNIFER: Well, what is he doing there? We have been waiting at the beach for two hours. We even went to the Deakin house. I had no idea you would be here. You promised to come down to the beach as soon as it was over.

SARAH: What? You barged in on the Deakin house in your beach things?

JENNIFER: Charlie, Sarah. We are talking about Charlie. What is going on?

SARAH: He's sulking.

JENNIFER: What has he got to sulk about?

SARAH: He behaved appallingly this afternoon.

JENNIFER: That's a lie. He never behaves appallingly and especially when he is out with you.

SARAH: He did today.

JENNIFER: What did he do?

SARAH: He treated the whole thing as if it were a complete joke.

JENNIFER: I very much doubt it. He never treats anything to do with music as a joke.

SARAH: Well, he behaved in a highly arrogant manner.

JENNIFER: I doubt that too.

SARAH: He certainly did. He was putting on airs and acting in a very superior way.

JENNIFER: I can't imagine that's true. Anyway, if he did seem to be 'putting on airs', you have only yourself to blame. You and Alice seem to have spent his whole life cultivating a profound sense of superiority in him. Good Heavens, you treat him like a little god around this house.

SARAH: That's not true.

JENNIFER: You do. You pamper him and you have a terrible tendency to neglect the others while you are doing it. Even your own.

SARAH: That's certainly not true.

Act II – Scene 2

JENNIFER: It is. Ever since the day he was born you seem to be dedicated to paying him as much attention as you can – good and bad. Why are you so obsessed with him?

SARAH: That is a ridiculous suggestion. If I do happen to pay him any particular attention, it's probably because he was the first. Isn't it natural for us to put a little more store in him than the others?

JENNIFER: Is it? I don't. I might tend towards my own a little more than any other children, but it never occurs to me to rank them according to some dubious principle of patrilineal precedence.

SARAH: Yes, well you have always been a little more evolved than the rest of us. But I don't think he minds the attention. In fact, I think he enjoys it.

JENNIFER: That's not the point.

SARAH: What is the point?

JENNIFER: I don't want him bothered with all that 'first child' responsibility. It is such a double-edged sword. Most of the time he can't put a foot wrong, but when he does, he's the worst in the world. I don't want him under all that pressure. I just want him to get on with his life and not feel he has to be House Captain over everything. I certainly don't want him to feel like he has to bear the brunt of the envy and disapproval of the others either. Why do you do that?

SARAH: I suppose because Granny does, and Jonathan seems to expect it.

JENNIFER: Why must you always be seeking to please them?

SARAH: I don't.

JENNIFER: You do. I see you. And I also see what a struggle it is for you. You seem to agonise over it all. It is like you always feel the need to set things in order. Order is very important to you. You make sure Charley is in order, then it's Jonathan, then it's Alice. Why do you put yourself under such a patently burdensome regime?

SARAH: You are exaggerating.

JENNIFER: I'm not.

SARAH: It is not a burden to me. It is just a natural concern for the welfare of my family.

JENNIFER: Implying that that is a concern that I don't share!

SARAH: I am not implying anything of the sort. And I resent you accusing me like this. It's very disturbing.

JENNIFER: Well, it's disturbing to me.

SARAH: What, a little intervention over Charles?

JENNIFER: It's not just about Charley.

Act II – Scene 2

SARAH: Well, who is it about?

JENNIFER: Well... well, we've been skirting about this for long enough. I know you have extraordinary feelings for Jonathan.

SARAH: Jennifer!

JENNIFER: Why shouldn't we talk about it?

SARAH: You are making it up.

JENNIFER: Come on. I know the stories. You have been in love with him since you were children.

SARAH: That's silly.

JENNIFER: It's not. It's the most natural thing in the world.

SARAH: I don't want to talk about this. It's really very wicked of you to bring it up.

JENNIFER: There's nothing wrong with it. I know you would never do anything about it. But I think it is particularly stupid to pretend it's not happening.

SARAH: You are his wife. Do you think it is appropriate to be discussing this?

JENNIFER: Why should I be left out of the discussion?

SARAH: What discussion?

JENNIFER: Come on Sarah. It's the family joke. Everyone knows you were engaged to him before he went off and come back a year later with me.

SARAH: Do they?

JENNIFER: I think at least three of your spinster aunts made it their business to tell me at the wedding.

SARAH: That was all gossip.

JENNIFER: Yes. It is just that in this case it happens to be true.

Pause.

SARAH: We weren't engaged. At least, nothing had been announced. It was just expected that we were to be married. So when he became engaged to you it gave all those awful Bainbridge women something to gossip about. And the Bainbridge men!

JENNIFER: Why did they think that?

SARAH: There was no particular reason. In those days we were always together so much that it was just assumed we would marry. I suppose I was somewhat naïve and encouraged them a little. But then again, I also had some encouragement.

JENNIFER: From Jonathan?

SARAH: Of course not. From Alice. The Bainbridge spinsters might have run with the 'word' but the idea was certainly Alice's.

JENNIFER: I see. That must have been uncomfortable.

Act II – Scene 2

SARAH: Actually, it was. I imagine I was a little bit in love with Jonathan, but, looking back on it, I feel as if I was pulled into the whole business. I think I always preferred Philip anyway. But then when you married Jonathan it looked like I got Philip as a consolation prize. More meat and drink for the Bainbridge gossip circle.

JENNIFER: You know I knew nothing about all this. Not until my wedding day.

SARAH: Yes, I know that.

JENNIFER: Did you even feel disappointed or resent me?

SARAH: No. Not really.

JENNIFER: Was Alice disappointed?

SARAH: I don't really know. Sorry to be so frank. It, like everything else with Alice, is something of a mystery.

JENNIFER: Surely I must have upset her plans?

SARAH: I'm not sure Alice thinks of her plans in those terms.

JENNIFER: What terms?

SARAH: Social alliances and judicious matches. There is always something more unconventional and wild about Alice's plans. She has no social self-consciousness at all. She has absolutely

	no business with tact. I suppose that is why I have become so obsessed with order – as you say.
JENNIFER:	Really? Are you so socially anxious?
SARAH:	I don't know. But I worry about this family and the way we live. There's something unruly about us – undisciplined. I have this terrible feeling that it is all going to end very badly.
JENNIFER:	Do you think we are that abnormal?
SARAH:	To be honest, I think abnormality would be a blessing in this family.

End Scene.

Act III: Scene 1

A tea shop. HENRY is sitting alone at a table. JENNIFER enters and spots him.

HENRY: Hello Mrs Bainbridge.

JENNIFER: Hello. Ah, there I have my excuse. Do you know this is now the third time we have met in two weeks and I have no idea about your name.

HENRY: That's shocking.

JENNIFER: It is. So, I am going to ignore the empty tables scattered about the place, insist on sitting with you and demand that you account for yourself.

HENRY: I advise caution. Didn't I tell you I am beyond the pale?

JENNIFER: You did, but we don't have to worry about that here. Have a look around. If you can honestly say that you actually know anyone in here, I will pay for your tea and scones. See? It's full of tourists. No one comes in here who actually lives here, I mean holidays here. It's one of the things I've realised about this place. It seems the locals avoid it like the plague. They think that if they come in here and order a cup of tea – when there is perfectly decent tea and hot water at home – that they will all go mad and break out in all sorts of welts and boils and poxes. Consequently, Mrs Millicent's tea shop is an oasis of calm, sanity and, above all, privacy.

HENRY: That is very noticing of you. Except, of course, everyone here knows that. So, if someone does see you ducking out after a quick pot of Lapsang Souchong and a slice of walnut cake, they will inevitably draw the conclusion that you are up to something. *[Whispering]* Not to mention the questionable discretion of Mrs Millicent herself.

JENNIFER: I will not have you casting aspersions on Mrs Millicent. You know the woman, she's an absolute darling. And discretion is her middle name.

HENRY: Even if Millicent isn't actually her surname.

JENNIFER: She won't tell. Her loyalty is to her customers. So as long as those people you speak of give this place a wide berth, one's privacy is protected.

HENRY: Now I am worried. You are scaring me. You have obviously thought a lot about this. I am staring to feel like I am part of a set-up.

JENNIFER: No. You don't get out of it that easily.

HENRY: What?

JENNIFER: Your name, sir?

HENRY: Newman.

Act III – Scene 1

JENNIFER: Mr, Sir, Lord or Reverend?

HENRY: Do I look like a clergyman or a knight or a titled foreigner?

JENNIFER: It's just that Newman is so pompous. It doesn't seem to suit you at all.

HENRY: I'll take that as a compliment. And it's Mr.

JENNIFER: Please do.

HENRY: Anyway, from whom are you seeking sanctuary? Not your children?

JENNIFER: No. My mother-in-law. My husband has, yet again, declined to come down to protect me from her, so I need to rediscover some energy against my next faux pas.

HENRY: I understand.

JENNIFER: Really. You know my mother-in-law?

HENRY: Only by reputation. But that's not what I mean. I mean I know mothers-in-law or at least the rumours about them.

JENNIFER: Do you have a mother-in-law?

HENRY: I had one once.

JENNIFER: And what was she like?

HENRY: Excellent in every way. We agreed on everything, except her daughter.

JENNIFER: Your wife?

HENRY: My former wife.

JENNIFER: Did she disapprove of you as a son-in-law?

HENRY: Only when I was nice to her daughter.

JENNIFER: What?

HENRY: That's what people don't really understand about getting on with mothers-in-law. It is not that they are trying to protect their children from you, it is that they are trying to protect you from their children. It's quite simple really.

JENNIFER: I will bear that in mind.

HENRY: Please don't. It will only confuse things. Tell me about your children. We are on much safer ground there.

JENNIFER: Are you really interested?

HENRY: I am. Of course I am. Why shouldn't I be? I have children of my own. You said your son is a talented pianist.

JENNIFER: No. I indicated that he can be unbearable without a piano.

HENRY: That amounts to the same thing. Don't be afraid that I will think you are bragging, if you admit he is a gifted musician. You see, I don't see that as any possible advantage in life. From my experience, anyone truly gifted at anything usually has a pretty hard time of it. Except me.

JENNIFER: What are you gifted at?

HENRY: Dilettanteism.

JENNIFER: Is that a gift?

HENRY: No. In fact, it is a study. I have lived so much of my life in fear of my actual gifts that I have had to work extremely hard at dilettanteism. As you can see, I have succeeded and, accordingly, I have preserved my sanity.

JENNIFER: Now I am worried.

HENRY: So he is gifted. Don't worry. I offer lessons.

JENNIFER: Thank you. But perhaps he is not all that gifted.

HENRY: Why do you say that?

JENNIFER: I think he has a reasonable sense of perspective over the whole business. The other day he was supposed to play Bach at the Deakin house and he took a look around the room and, instead, offered up a selection from *The Mikado*.

HENRY: But that is the proof of genius. In fact, it may well be a summary of the life and work of Sir Arthur Sullivan himself.

JENNIFER: Yes, but it's hardly a gift. More of an instinct.

HENRY: All of which goes to show you have nothing to worry about. What about his sister?

JENNIFER: Tomboy. Detests dolls and dresses and just wants to play cricket.

HENRY: More genius. It sounds like you have done a wonderful job.

JENNIFER: Despite the absentee father?

HENRY: Don't be too hard on him. He is obviously a gentleman of some taste and good sense to be so unavailable during school holidays at the Bainbridge household.

JENNIFER: You sound like you know him? You men all stick together.

HENRY: I know of him. But I am not apologising for him. Quite obviously he has complete confidence in your ability to handle his mother and that is the highest compliment any husband can pay his wife.

JENNIFER: I'll telephone him tomorrow and he'll probably tell me you know him from the bank and that you went to school with his father.

HENRY: Would it alarm you if I asked you not to do that?

JENNIFER: No. It would intrigue me, not alarm me.

HENRY: That is almost as bad.

JENNIFER: Why? Are you an outlaw?

Act III – Scene 1

HENRY: I told you. I am beyond the pale with that family and a great many others of their acquaintance. Of course nothing would come of it if you did mention me. It is just that, if you did, we could never meet again. Now you may not think anything of it, but it would be a great disappointment to me personally if that happened. I don't mean you any bother, but I do enjoy talking to you. Please believe me when I say that. I have every confidence in friendships between men and women. It is just in my position, I have to spend much of the day being avoided by people, so I do occasionally crave some conversation.

JENNIFER: What on earth did you do?

HENRY: Now that would alarm you and to tell you would commit you to an unwanted intimacy that, no doubt, you will have no use for by the end of the summer. Needless to say, it is not murder or anything criminal, not in the legal sense any way. Come and ask me if you do happen to betray me and I will tell you the real story.

JENNIFER: So do you think it is possible for two people to be friends, both knowing that there is a perpetually unexplained elephant in the room?

HENRY: Friends, acquaintances, lovers, enemies... the unexplained elephant in the room seems to me to be the basis of almost all really significant relationships.

End Scene.

Act III: Scene 2

The Bainbridge house sitting room later that day.

JENNIFER has returned and is taking things off.

JENNIFER: Sophie! Charlie! Where are you? *[Pause]* Charlie! Where are you? *[Pause]* Is there anyone here at all?

ALICE: *[Off]* I am. Do stop yelling.

JENNIFER: Where is everyone? It's time we started dinner.

Enter ALICE.

ALICE: They've gone.

JENNIFER: Where?

ALICE: To the Smithers.

JENNIFER: That's in Geelong. When did they go? They won't be back for ages.

ALICE: They won't be back at all. Not this evening.

JENNIFER: What do you mean?

ALICE: They left just after lunch and they intend to stay there for the night.

JENNIFER: What on earth are you talking about?

ALICE: Sarah's been talking about it for weeks.

JENNIFER: About what?

ALICE: Taking the children to stay at the Smithers.

JENNIFER: She said nothing to me about it. I don't want my children staying at the Smithers, or anywhere else for that matter, without my knowledge.

ALICE: I wouldn't worry. I am sure they will have a delightful time. Although staying in other people's houses has never had any appeal for me.

JENNIFER: I had absolutely no idea about it. Really this is intolerable. Sarah had no business to just take them off like that. When did this come up? Did she discuss it with you?

ALICE: I said I thought it was a good idea. Give you some time to yourself.

JENNIFER: I don't understand you people. Why do you all keep doing this? What on earth makes you think you can just do anything you like with my children and not consult me.

ALICE: They are my grandchildren.

JENNIFER: So, you would simply allow your mother-in-law to suit herself when it came to your children?

ALICE: I never had a mother-in-law.

JENNIFER: Well, can't you reflect for a minute on what it might have been like if you did?

ALICE: Most disagreeable I would imagine.

JENNIFER: Yes. Quite.

ALICE: You don't need to take that tone with me. It wasn't my idea. Sarah seemed to think you had agreed and I merely thought it was a good idea. I am not in the habit of ordering Sarah about one way or another.

JENNIFER: Only because she does what you want without it. I have really had enough of all this. I want you to be perfectly clear that I don't want any decisions about my children to be made by anyone but me. And I intend to say the same thing to Sarah.

ALICE: Very well. Although I think you are making far too much of it. They will be back by lunch time tomorrow.

JENNIFER: But don't you agree that this is all quite irregular?

ALICE: At my time of life, nothing appears irregular. At least not to my experience. So, I don't agree. But Sarah certainly does not agree. She thinks this sort of thing – rushing about in public conveniences and staying in strange people's houses – is the height of normality. Therefore, nothing slightly unusual that she does to achieve it can ever be irregular.

JENNIFER: I have spoken to her about it.

ALICE: Indeed?

JENNIFER: Yes. She seems obsessed with the idea that we are an undisciplined family.

ALICE: In my experience most families are undisciplined. That is why they huddle together so tenaciously, in a desperate attempt to hold off the chaos. Do you think we are undisciplined?

JENNIFER: I don't really know what that means.

ALICE: For Sarah it means me.

JENNIFER: What do you mean?

ALICE: Poor Sarah has spent so much of her life trying to be my daughter-in-law that now she is well ensconced in the position she finds its utterly disgusting.

JENNIFER: Disgusting? Is that really the word?

ALICE: Distasteful at least. You see she has never really reconciled herself to my style of life.

JENNIFER: What is your style of life?

ALICE: My ménage.

JENNIFER: I can't see anything so disgusting about it. You are hardly the only woman in the world living apart from her husband. For goodness sake, I am starting to think we all live like that, given that Jonathan and Philip are never here.

ALICE: She thinks we are cursed.

Act III – Scene 2

JENNIFER: Why should she think that?

ALICE: Because of my reputation, I suppose.

JENNIFER: I don't know anything about that. What is your reputation 'Granny'?

ALICE: I believe I am referred to as a 'hard woman'.

JENNIFER: Why?

ALICE: Do you know, no one has ever really asked me that. Some people think they know. Fewer people actually know. But no one has ever dared to ask.

JENNIFER: It is not exactly an easy thing to discuss.

ALICE: People don't seem to mind holding the most abominable opinions about me, or what I am supposed to have done, but they just don't want to express them.

JENNIFER: Do you feel the need to talk about it?

ALICE: Not in the least.

JENNIFER: Well, I suppose that's it then. *[Long pause]* Are you sure you are not just saying that, but really, all the time, you are wanting to talk about it?

ALICE: Quite sure. I am not a Roman Catholic. I am immune from the delights of the confessional. Everything else is just gossip and, in time, that is worth precisely nothing.

End Scene.

Act IV: Scene 1

It is some weeks later. JENNIFER and HENRY are standing in the shallows of a delightful but unfashionable, and therefore deserted, part of the beach.

JENNIFER: Do you think it safe for me to be alone with you on this part of the beach?

HENRY: Quite safe. Haven't you noticed? We have been standing here for at least fifteen minutes and no one at all has appeared.

JENNIFER: That is not quite true. I am sure I saw a small party poke their nose around those rocks a few minutes ago.

HENRY: Yes, but they took a look at the general absence and decided to have none of it.

JENNIFER: I can't see why no one comes to this part of the beach. It's much nicer than around the corner where everyone seems to congregate.

HENRY: Misery loves a crowd.

JENNIFER: Well, I am glad. It's lovely here.

Pause.

HENRY: What news of your husband?

JENNIFER: He was here.

HENRY: Really?

JENNIFER: About a week ago. Just for a few days.

HENRY: That must have been nice!

JENNIFER: It wasn't particularly.

HENRY: I'm sorry.

JENNIFER: He's never here and I am not there. Living with his family is like having that less congenial bit of your partner, that you usually manage to overlook, full-time rather than it just flaring up intermittently. As the summer's gone on we have been apart so much that establishing any positive continuity seems impossible.

HENRY: The summer will end. There will be time for that.

JENNIFER: Perhaps. But you don't make it any easier.

HENRY: Yes?

JENNIFER: You are the model of positive continuity. I am not sure I want the summer to end.

HENRY: Oh, it's easy for me to seem that. You're surrounded by troubles. All I have to do is swan in occasionally and make some polite and mildly diverting conversation and it all seems like an oasis of civilised living.

JENNIFER: It's more than that.

Act IV – Scene 1

HENRY: Possibly. But I am sure it's not quite what you think it is.

JENNIFER: I've embarrassed you, I think?

HENRY: Not at all. I understand you quite well, I think. And I feel something very similar. But it is not as simple or conventional as either of us could really imagine. But yes, I am glad. And I certainly feel it too.

JENNIFER: Is that my dismissal?

HENRY: No. I suppose not. Although it could be. There's really no call for idle chatter now.

JENNIFER: Yes. You're quite right. No call whatsoever.

They continue to look out to sea and the lights fade.

Act IV: Scene 2

*The dining/sitting room later that evening.
JENNIFER is sitting enjoying her solitude.
Soon SARAH enters.*

SARAH: Are you all right?

JENNIFER: Perfectly all right.

SARAH: You are not unwell? Sitting here all on your own.

JENNIFER: I assure you I am perfectly well.

SARAH: Jennifer, I know about that man.

JENNIFER: What do you know?

SARAH: I know about that man you've been speaking to. I have heard all about it.

JENNIFER: He's called Mr Newman.

SARAH: I know, Mr Henry Newman.

JENNIFER: What, you've had your spies looking out for me? I must say they have taken their time. If they had really been doing their job, you would have found out months ago. We have hardly been hiding behind bushes. But you needn't worry. It is so respectable it's almost questionable.

SARAH: He's Jonathan's father.

JENNIFER: What?

SARAH: His real name is Bainbridge and he's Jonathan and Philip's father.

JENNIFER: Of course he is.

SARAH: You knew?

JENNIFER: Not at all. But it makes sense now you tell me.

SARAH: He approached me too. In Melbourne. In fact, I went to see him. You can't really hold it against him; he is desperate to know about his children, and his grandchildren.

JENNIFER: What would I hold against him? He hasn't hurt me or my children. He hasn't swindled me out of money or compromised my reputation.

SARAH: Of course not.

JENNIFER: All he has done is talked to me. And listened to me when I talked.

SARAH: He is certainly very charming.

JENNIFER: I don't think so. Do you? I haven't found him charming at all. Why should he need to be charming? It makes sense that he might want to know me and get some information about Jonathan and the children. But he hasn't resorted to charm in order to do it.

SARAH: You must be shocked.

Act IV – Scene 2

JENNIFER: No, I'm not. As I said, it makes perfect sense. Anyway, who told you about me and my 'man'?

SARAH: Just some local women I know.

JENNIFER: I hope they won't go gossiping about it? I'd hate to think how really awful that would be for him.

SARAH: And not for you?

JENNIFER: No. Not for me.

SARAH: Well, you don't know. Anyway, I put a stop to all that.

JENNIFER: That was kind. How did you do it?

SARAH: I told them you knew it was the boys' father and that you had approached him – which is why he is daring to show his face down here in the first place.

JENNIFER: That was far thinking of you Sarah.

SARAH: You are reacting in the strangest way. Are you sure you are all right?

JENNIFER: Of course.

SARAH: You're not upset. He didn't... do anything... to upset you?

JENNIFER: Not at all.

SARAH: You haven't fallen for him?

JENNIFER: Would it be so extraordinary if I did? Until a minute ago I had no natural reason not to.

SARAH: Jennifer!

JENNIFER: Never mind. I didn't fall for him. Not like that. But I did talk to him and, as I say, he talked to me. We have come to understand each other a great deal.

SARAH: I suppose that's good. In a way. Although I doubt much good can come of it.

JENNIFER: Why do you say that?

SARAH: Just because you know him now – we know him now – it can hardly mean anything is going to change.

JENNIFER: You think so.

SARAH: I know so.

JENNIFER: Do you?

SARAH: I do.

JENNIFER: You seem to know everything, Sarah.

SARAH: I can assure you I don't.

JENNIFER: Well, you certainly know more than me.

SARAH: I don't know that is exactly true. Perhaps it's just that I have been around longer.

Act IV – Scene 2

JENNIFER: Well, I think someone had better tell me exactly what I want to know about this family right now, or I am going to pack my bags, take my children, present myself at that man's house and offer to live with him, indefinitely, and on any terms and conditions that he requires.

SARAH: Jennifer!

JENNIFER: Does that alarm you?

SARAH: It's preposterous.

JENNIFER: Not it's not. I am living in this house under much the same conditions. It's not preposterous at all. If you don't tell me I will go and speak to Alice and propose the same arrangement.

SARAH: You won't get anything from her.

JENNIFER: What, even if I threaten to walk out and take my family to live with her husband?

SARAH: I have told you, she won't blink an eyelash. She's beyond scandal.

JENNIFER: Well, you're not. I know that. So, you had better tell me. Or don't you trust me? Don't I belong in the circle?

SARAH: It's not like that.

JENNIFER: Well, tell me what you know.

SARAH: Very little, actually. As you know, Alice says nothing. The boys were too young to know much. I think their father had pretty much left by the time Jonathan was ten or eleven. I gather Henry came home from the first war, collected his things and pretty much moved out all at once – or he was kicked out.

JENNIFER: Which was it?

SARAH: Your guess is as good as mine. You know what she's like. Come to think of it you know what he's like too.

JENNIFER: I can certainly see why anyone would want to put some distance into their relationship with Alice.

SARAH: Apparently, she had her reasons too.

JENNIFER: And what were they?

SARAH: Other women. Apparently, there was some scandal involving one of his parishioners.

JENNIFER: Parishioners? He is a minister?

SARAH: He was a minister.

JENNIFER: He never said so.

SARAH: I gather it was in the papers and there was something about a court case.

JENNIFER: What about? They're not divorced, are they?

SARAH: No. I suppose it was about money. I asked Jonathan once and he just sidestepped the issues. But I know he was involved, because they made him go into court and give evidence.

JENNIFER: For Heaven's sake.

SARAH: But, as I say, I don't know. It's all just gossip really. When you think about it though, how could it be anything else?

JENNIFER: What do you mean?

SARAH: Well, when you have all the key protagonists in such a state of bewilderment about the truth of their own lives, how can anyone else possibility know the reality of it?

End Scene.

ACT IV: SCENE 3

A courtroom scene twenty years earlier.

JENNIFER: *[As press woman]* Mrs Alice Eleanor Bainbridge, aged 45 years of Rothwell Street, Ascot Vale, petitioned to Mr Justice Lowe, the third civil court yesterday, April 26, 1927, for a judicial separation from Henry Ernest Bainbridge, aged 46 years, whose address was given as Cavendish House, Burwood Road, Hawthorne, clergyman, on the grounds of desertion. The marriage took place on November 26, 1905 at North Essendon. The ceremony was performed by the Rev. H. G. Bainbridge, according to the rites of the Presbyterian Church. There are two sons of the marriage.

ALICE: I was born at Warrnambool. Immediately after our marriage the respondent and I lived at Fitzgerald Street, South Yarra, where we remained for two and a half years. We then removed to Clarinda Road, Essendon, where we remained for two and a half years. We then moved to Newry Street, North Fitzroy, where we remained for about eight months. During this time my husband was supported by me out of my income, and in addition I paid for his fees to attend the Melbourne University. He was ordained as a clergyman, and we then went to Fiji, where we remained for about two and a half years. On our return to Victoria we went to Leongatha, where we remained for about the same time. My husband then went to the war, and returned home in February

1919. Till June 1919, we went to live in Ballarat, everything had been most satisfactory. I had a private income of £200 a year, and up to the time we went to Fiji it was used by me for the upkeep of the house. When we went to Fiji the respondent began to earn money, and from that time I paid at first two-thirds, and, ultimately one-half of the total upkeep of the house. From the time we arrived in Ballarat our life has been most unhappy. Almost immediately on arrival the respondent met a Mrs Hook. He paid great attention to her. She was continuously at the manse, and although I complained to him about it he would not ask her to discontinue her visits. He repeatedly visited Mrs Hook at her home, and particularly while her husband was at business. I asked him not to visit her but he continued to do so. I bought a motor-car for the respondent. Whenever he took me out he always took Mrs Hook, and had her in the front seat. I suggested on one occasion that we should take another woman out, but he refused, and would not take me out in the car for six weeks afterwards. The respondent was talked about so much in Ballarat that the church secretary [Mr Watson], Mr Hook, the respondent, and Mrs Hook had a discussion, with the result that my husband promised not to visit Mrs Hook again unless her husband was present. Within four days the respondent was visiting Mrs Hook again in the absence of her husband. My husband taught Mrs Hook to play tennis, and afterwards played with her, and no one else. He always walked to and

Act IV – Scene 3

from the tennis court with her. Although I asked him to walk with me and other women he would not do so.

Pause.

SARAH: *[As Justice Lowe]* Please continue, Mrs Bainbridge.

ALICE: I own a house at Point Lonsdale, and I used to go there with my children for the Christmas holidays. While I would be at Point Lonsdale the respondent was continuously in the company of Mrs Hook, and when he joined me at Point Lonsdale, he brought with him Mr and Mrs Hook, who stayed at an adjoining boarding-house. Every morning the respondent and Mrs Hook would go for a swim, and although it was exceptionally cold, they would be away for about an hour and a half. When we were leaving Ballarat the societies of Ballarat decided to give us a presentation and collected about £35. It was handed to the respondent for us, but he refused to give me any of it. He also sold about £50 worth of furniture and kept the proceeds. He gave Mrs Hook a gold bangle when he was leaving. From Ballarat we went to Auburn, where we remained until Christmas 1924. At this time my husband treated me with great coldness. On Christmas Eve when I was leaving for a health trip to Great Britain he come down to the vessel, merely raised his hat and said 'goodbye.' While in England the respondent wrote his sister a letter that made it impossible for me to return to him. On my return to Australia he made the following conditions before he would take me back: I was to withdraw all insinuations against him; acknowledge his friendship with Mrs Hook; make a will in his favour; pay down a lump sum [about £250]; and guarantee to pay half the upkeep of the house and family. Since December 1924, he has never offered to make a home for me, nor has he offered to provide for my maintenance.

JENNIFER: *[As Press Woman]* Mr Woolf, appearing for the petitioner, said that an appearance had been entered on behalf of the respondent, but no answer had been filed. Mr Justice Lowe said:

SARAH: *[As Justice Lowe]* I have read the affidavit. I wonder why this mass of information has been set out. It seems to point to different grounds from those upon which the petition was lodged.

JENNIFER: *[As Press Woman]* Mr Woolf said that the petitioner had a well-founded belief of impropriety but had no direct evidence of it. The conditions imposed by the respondent were so unreasonable that the petitioner was perfectly justified in refusing to comply with them.

SARAH: *[As Justice Lowe]* I do not see any statement that she has refused these conditions.

JENNIFER: *[As Press Woman]* Mr Woolf said that the petitioner had gone to England, broken down in health, and when she returned the respondent had met her in the city. That was on July 10, 1925. The had tea at the Wattles. They met later by appointment at Flinders Street Station and walked up and down Alexandra Avenue. The petitioner showed him a letter that he had written to his sister and asked him what the terms were to which he had referred. The terms were those mentioned in the affidavit. He said:

HENRY has entered just prior.

HENRY: You see my solicitors.

JENNIFER: *[As Press Woman]* She replied:

ALICE: This is a matter for us and not for any solicitor.

JENNIFER: *[As Press Woman]* Finally, he stated what the terms were. She said that she could not agree to them as it meant going back to the misery she had suffered for the last five years. Bainbridge refused to give this other woman up. He said:

HENRY: She has stuck to me when everyone else has been against me.

ALICE: *[To Justice Lowe]* We were married by my husband's father. My maiden name was Fraser. My husband promised his brother that he would not speak to this woman again, that he would write to his father and become reconciled to him, and that he would write and tell Mrs Hook so. When he came to see me at Point Lonsdale later, he looked defiantly at me, and his face was as black as thunder. He said:

HENRY: I have been considering things. You can live with me on my own conditions.

ALICE: *[To Justice Lowe]* At that time Mrs Hook was at Point Lonsdale. They had travelled together from Geelong. Mr Hook was employed by a firm of men's outfitters.

SARAH: *[As Justice Lowe]* When you went to England did you provide the means yourself?

ALICE: *[To Justice Lowe]* Every penny of it. I was very anxious to keep on the home we were renting in Melbourne, but he refused to do so. He would not allow me to pay the rent myself.

SARAH: *[As Justice Lowe]* When you left him did you part on friendly terms?

ALICE: *[To Justice Lowe]* We had not been friendly for months. As I was walking to the ship, he was walking away from it. He simply raised his hat and went on.

SARAH: *[As Justice Lowe]* Why do you not want a divorce instead of a judicial separation?

ALICE: *[To Justice Lowe]* Because I do not believe in divorce. Those who are married I believe are joined for ever.

SARAH: *[As Justice Lowe]* Then why do you want a judicial separation?

Act IV – Scene 3

ALICE: *[To Justice Lowe]* Because my husband said that he would go to Canada and get a divorce there. I did not want my name to go down to my children as a woman who had been divorced.

JENNIFER: *[As Press Woman]* Mr Watson, Secretary of the Presbyterian Church in Ballarat, said, "During the discussion that took place when the respondent and Mrs Hook were present, Mrs Hook said, 'I know I am the fly in the ointment, and that all the other women of the church are jealous.'" Jonathan Peter Bainbridge, son of the petitioner and respondent, said:

JONATAHN has entered just prior.

JONATHAN: While we were living at Ballarat my father used to ring up Mrs Hook every morning.

SARAH: *[As Justice Lowe]* I suppose that your father rang up other members of the congregation as well?

JONATHAN: Yes, but not the same parishioner every morning. *[Pause]*

JENNIFER: *[As Press Woman]* Mr Justice Lowe said that it was a most extraordinary case. He proposed to grant a decree on the uncorroborated evidence of the petitioner. There would be a decree for judicial separation, with costs on the grounds of desertion. He would reserve the question of alimony.

Fade Lights.

Act V: Scene 1

The dining/sitting room, in the days following act four: scene two. SARAH is setting the table for afternoon tea as ALICE enters, having returned from a walk.

SARAH: How was your walk?

ALICE: Exactly the same as every other day since I came here and built this house. I am like you in that respect only, Sarah. I appreciate order and regularity in my afternoon walk.

SARAH: Surely you had to vary it a little during the war, Granny? I can't imagine the Army let you wander at will around the lighthouse and the point.

ALICE: Then you mistake the scope of my influence, young woman.

SARAH: Oh, I don't know that.

ALICE: Why are you only setting tea for four?

SARAH: Because there are only four of us.

ALICE: Four?

SARAH: I sent the children to the Deakin house for the afternoon. Charles obviously made quite an impression last time, so they have asked him back. I said the others could go along with him provided they kept their vocal contributions to strict unison. Sophie's harmonising has become far too Byzantine of late, don't you think?

ALICE: Sophie is Byzantine. But who is the fourth?

SARAH: I have invited an acquaintance of Jennifer's. A delightful man. His name is Mr Newman.

ALICE: Sarah!

SARAH: So, you know him?

ALICE: There's absolutely nothing I don't know about Mr Newman – as you well know. Why have you invited him here?

SARAH: Well, Jennifer knows all about him too. She does now at least. And I thought it was time we put an end to all this pointless mystery. You see, Granny, I've had enough. Now that Jennifer knows the basics, like me, I think it's high time we sorted out the details.

ALICE: You mean the gossip?

SARAH: No. I don't want the gossip. I mean the details of how we are going to go on in this family by making some sort of reconciliation with the past.

ALICE: For the sake of your social position.

SARAH: No. For the children's sake. You see they don't have any concern for your petty bedroom squabbles. They simply want to know who their grandparents are. And I think they

Act V – Scene 1

have a right to. Besides the whole situation has become quite unbearable. I saw you that day when Charles found the trunk with your husband's name on it. I think it was one of the most pitiable things I have ever seen.

ALICE: It is one thing to ease the children into some understanding of their paternity, but it's another thing to have him here in the house. I will never agree to that. If that man tries to come through the front door I will close it in his face.

SARAH: You won't, because if you do, I will take my children away and never let them come anywhere near you or this house again. Jennifer will do the same. You see, we're taking over Granny. I know how to do this. I have been watching you for years. And I am not willing to be subject to it any longer. So, if you want to see your grandchildren grow up, as I intend that your ex-husband will, you will participate in this process – enthusiastically.

ALICE: How dare you dictate terms to me in my own house.

SARAH: Well, it's my house too. I live here and so do my children. If you can't abide me asserting myself then I will leave, but I will be leaving on those terms.

ALICE: I never thought you impudent before.

SARAH: You were gravely mistaken.

ALICE: It won't work, you know. He won't come. Especially if he knows I am here.

SARAH: Well, he is coming. In fact, he said that, above everything else, he wanted to apologise to Jennifer.

ALICE: Jennifer?

SARAH: It seems he feels he has been less than honest with her.

ALICE: That has never stopped him doing or not doing anything before.

SARAH: I think you are quite wrong. But we'll see.

JENNIFER enters.

JENNIFER: So, Granny, you know about Sarah's cunning plan?

ALICE: It is not cunning, it's foolhardy.

JENNIFER: You think?

ALICE: I know that man. I also know myself and a good deal more about the world than you do. Doubtless in your minds this whole idea of 'reconciliation', as you call it Sarah, is some sort of romantic inclination towards a longed for Utopia of family harmony. You have never considered the possibility that it might be, in any way, harmful. Nor have you considered

Act V – Scene 1

the prospect that your little scenario is simply playful – the mischievous product of a bored and lazy sensibility.

SARAH: That's unkind.

ALICE: Tell me frankly. Doesn't the staging of this little scene between a damaged and estranged former husband and wife titillate you just a bit?

SARAH: Not at all.

ALICE: You are not honest. I know you think I am bedevilled with mystification and self-delusion, but you obviously have just as much capacity for self-delusion as anyone. [*Pause*] As for your scruples about the restitution of this family, I can see for you all it might seem like a 'nice' idea. But the means by which I could possibly become reconciled to that man can only be obscure and fantastical to you at best. You have no idea what took place between us. I have said almost nothing on the subject and I very much doubt you have been bold enough to probe him. One thing I will tell you, now that you have seen fit to bring on this nasty little affair, is that any confrontation between us, even in the most seemingly polite and cordial terms, can only be, for me, disastrous and painful. And given five minutes' notice and absolutely no time to prepare myself, the likelihood of this encounter being any use or benefit to you, your children, or to me, is negligible. So at the risk of never seeing my grandchildren again, or you Jennifer, or you Sarah, I prefer to withdraw.

SARAH: You're quite sure about that Granny?

ALICE: *[Departing]* Given what people are, Sarah, I doubt it will happen that way. But sometimes, just sometimes, it's exactly the sort of scenario I dream about.

She leaves.

JENNIFER: What do you make of that?

SARAH: Not much. She is just calling my bluff.

JENNIFER: In what sense?

SARAH: He's not coming at all. I never asked him.

JENNIFER: Really?

SARAH: I'm not mad. They would have probably tried to kill each another.

JENNIFER: Did they really hate each other that much?

SARAH: Eventually. From what I hear they were quite the glamour couple in their day. Passionately in love and passionately jealous of each other's brilliance and accomplishment.

JENNIFER: Well, I'm not sure there's much of that left in Henry. But 'passionate' is certainly the mot juste for Alice. In fact, I have never known her to do anything in any other way. *[Pause]* Do you think she really knows he's not coming?

SARAH: I have no doubt whatsoever.

Lights fade to the sound of Beethoven's **Appassionata** *sonata, first movement.*

Curtain.

www.ingramcontent.com/pod-product-compliance
Lightning Source LLC
Chambersburg PA
CBHW071410080526
44587CB00017B/3234